PIANO • VOCAL • GUITAR

THE BEST OF TOBY KEITH

T5-CVQ-964

ISBN 0-634-09610-9

HAL•LEONARD®
CORPORATION
7777 W. BLUEMOUND RD. P.O. BOX 13819 MILWAUKEE. WI 53213

Visit Hal Leonard Online at
www.halleonard.com

BEER FOR MY HORSES

Words and Music by TOBY KEITH
and SCOTT EMERICK

COURTESY OF THE
RED, WHITE AND BLUE
(The Angry American)

Words and Music by
TOBY KEITH

Slowly, freely

A-mer-i-can girls _ and A-mer-i-can guys, _ we'll al-ways

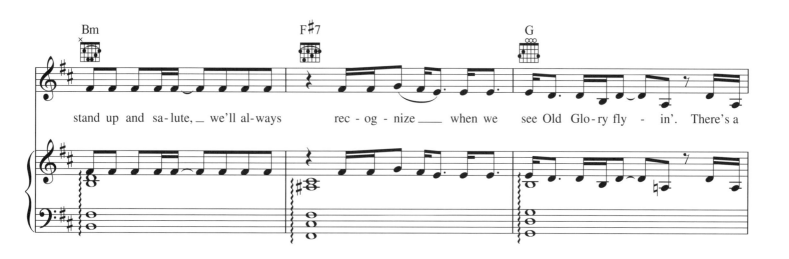

stand up and sa-lute, _ we'll al-ways rec-og-nize ___ when we see Old Glo-ry fly - in'. There's a

lot of men dead _ so we can sleep in peace at night when we lay down our head. _

you hear Moth - er Free - dom start ring- in' her bell, __ and it -'ll feel ___ like the whole __ wide world __

___ is rain - in' down on ___ you. ___

Brought to you cour - te - sy of the Red, White and Blue.

Guitar solo

DOES THAT BLUE MOON EVER SHINE ON YOU

Words and Music by
TOBY KEITH

Day by day ___

we let love just walk a-way, ___ and I'll be the first to say ___
you were right there all the time. ___ I could search and nev-er find ___

___ I was glad to see ___ it go. And day ___ by day, ___
___ some-one ___ that does me like ___ you do. Here's ___ a part ___

DREAM WALKIN'

Words and Music by TOBY KEITH
and CHUCK CANNON

GETCHA SOME

Words and Music by TOBY KEITH
and CHUCK CANNON

HE AIN'T WORTH MISSING

Words and Music by
TOBY KEITH

I'M JUST TALKIN' ABOUT TONIGHT

Words and Music by SCOTTY EMERICK
and TOBY KEITH

I'M SO HAPPY I CAN'T STOP CRYING

Music and Lyrics by
STING

42

A LITTLE LESS TALK
AND A LOT MORE ACTION

Words and Music by KEITH HINTON
and JIMMY ALAN STEWART

lit-tle less talk __ and a lot more ac-tion.

Guitar solo

SHOULD'VE BEEN A COWBOY

Words and Music by
TOBY KEITH

Moderate Country Rock

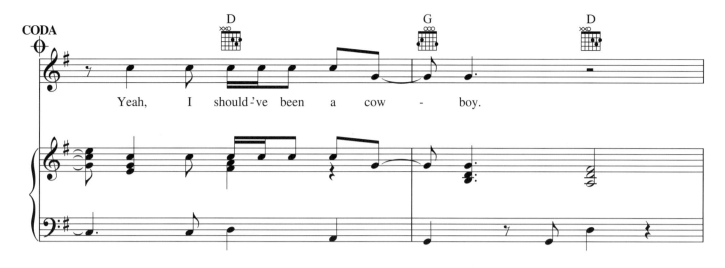

Yeah, I should-'ve been a cow - boy.

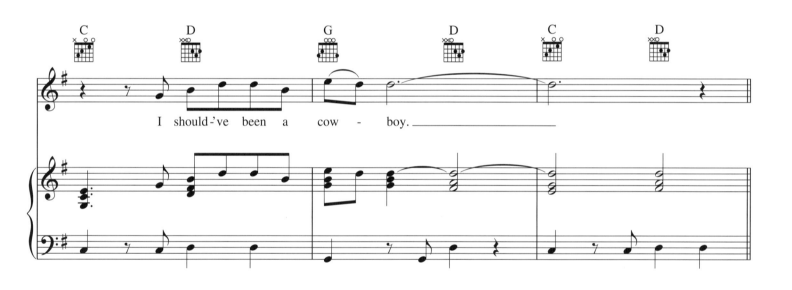

I should-'ve been a cow - boy. _____

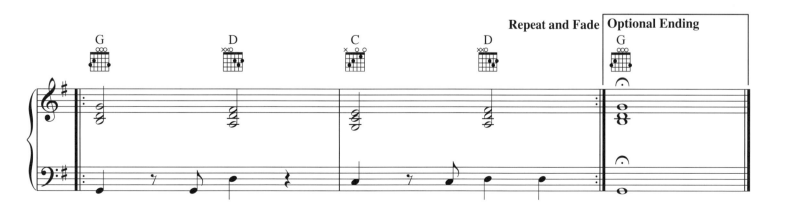

STAYS IN MEXICO

Words and Music by
TOBY KEITH

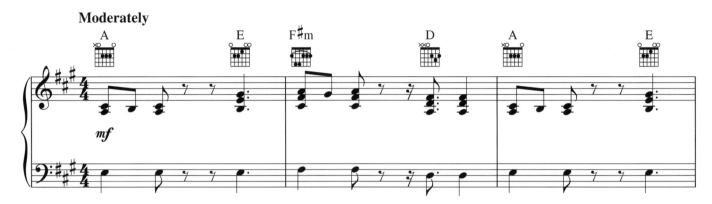

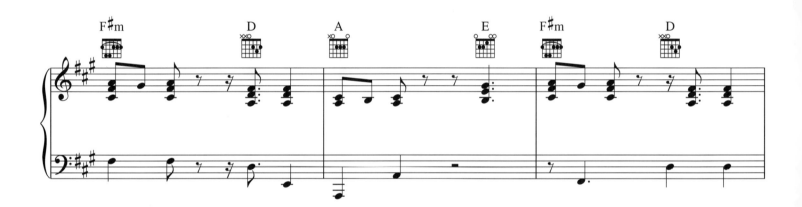

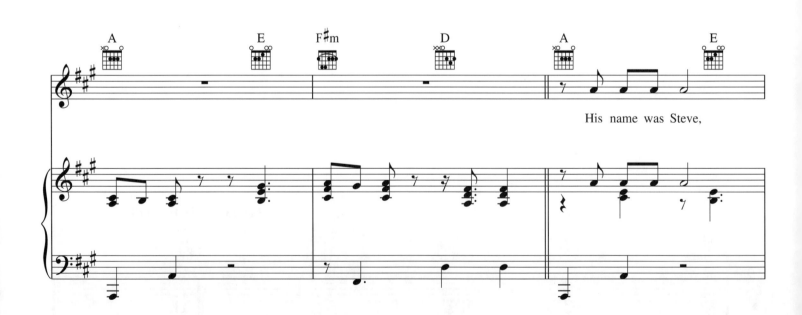

His name was Steve,

WE WERE IN LOVE

Words and Music by ALLEN SHAMBLIN
and CHUCK CANNON

WHO'S THAT MAN

Words and Music by
TOBY KEITH

WHO'S YOUR DADDY?

Words and Music by
TOBY KEITH

Moderate Honky-Tonk

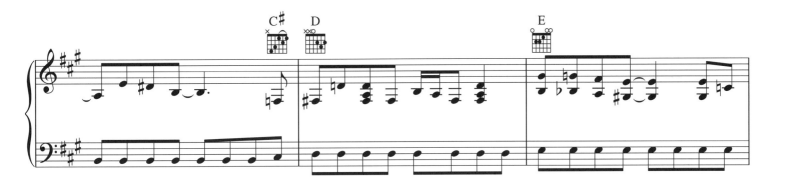

WISH I DIDN'T KNOW NOW

Words and Music by
TOBY KEITH

D.S. al Coda

Yeah, I wish some - how __ I did - n't know now _____

what I did - n't know __ then. ____

YOU AIN'T MUCH FUN

Words and Music by TOBY KEITH
and CARL GOFF, JR.

CODA

quit drink - in'.

Yeah, I so - bered up _____ and

I got to think - in', girl, you ain't much fun since I _____ quit drink - in'.